T0413296

TOOLS FOR CAREGIVERS

- **F&P LEVEL:** C
- **WORD COUNT:** 30

- **CURRICULUM CONNECTIONS:** machines

Skills to Teach

- **HIGH-FREQUENCY WORDS:** a, big, has, I, is, it, see
- **CONTENT WORDS:** blade, bulldozer, dig, drive, push, rippers, tracks
- **PUNCTUATION:** periods
- **WORD STUDY:** digraph /sh/ (*push*); /k/, spelled *ck* (*tracks*); long /e/, spelled *ee* (*see*)
- **TEXT TYPE:** information report

Before Reading Activities

- Read the title and give a simple statement of the main idea.
- Have students "walk" through the book and talk about what they see in the pictures.
- Introduce new vocabulary by having students predict the first letter and locate the word in the text.
- Discuss any unfamiliar concepts that are in the text.

After Reading Activities

Bulldozers push. Explain to readers that the "sh" in *push* is a digraph. A digraph is two letters put together to make a combined sound. Ask readers to name other words that use the "sh" diagraph. Write their answers on the board.

Tadpole Books are published by Jump!, 5357 Penn Avenue South, Minneapolis, MN 55419, www.jumplibrary.com

Copyright ©2025 Jump. International copyright reserved in all countries. No part of this book may be reproduced in any form without written permission from the publisher.

Editor: Jenna Gleisner   **Designer:** Emma Almgren-Bersie

Photo Credits: SweetyMommy/iStock, cover; mgkaya/iStock, 1; Stefan11/Dreamstime, 2tl, 12–13; Photoerick/Dreamstime, 2tr, 10–11; Mr. Tempter/Shutterstock, 2ml, 6–7; Yevhen 11/Shutterstock, 2mr, 14–15; kadmy/iStock, 2bl, 8–9; Shark9208888/Shutterstock, 2br, 4–5; Maksim Safaniuk/Shutterstock, 3; Robert J. Beyers II/Shutterstock, 16.

Library of Congress Cataloging-in-Publication Data
Names: Gleisner, Jenna Lee, author.
Title: Bulldozers / by Jenna Lee Gleisner.
Description: Minneapolis, MN: Jump!, Inc., [2025]
Series: Machines on the move | Includes index.
Audience: Ages 3–6
Identifiers: LCCN 2024021006 (print)
LCCN 2024021007 (ebook)
ISBN 9798892135863 (hardcover)
ISBN 9798892135870 (paperback)
ISBN 9798892135887 (ebook)
Subjects: LCSH: Bulldozers—Juvenile literature. | Earthmoving machinery—Juvenile literature.
Classification: LCC TA735 .G55723 2025 (print)
LCC TA735 (ebook)
DDC 629.225—dc23/eng/20240513
LC record available at https://lccn.loc.gov/2024021006
LC ebook record available at https://lccn.loc.gov/2024021007

BULLDOZERS

by Jenna Lee Gleisner

TABLE OF CONTENTS

tadpole books

WORDS TO KNOW

blade

dig

drive

push

rippers

tracks

PUSH

I see a bulldozer.

3

track

It has tracks.

I see it drive.

ripper

It has rippers.

I see it dig.

blade

It has a blade.

It is big.

I see it push.

LET'S REVIEW!

Bulldozers are big machines! What is this bulldozer pushing?

INDEX